I Wrote a Book

❧ For You ❧

BY: _____

_____

_____

You are special to me because

I like when we go to

My favorite thing about you is

If I could fly, I would take you to the

When we are together, we like to

You have a great

You are so

I like it when you

If I could cook
anything in the
world, I would
make you a

My favorite food to eat with you is

Our favorite show to watch together is

I know you love me because

You make the best

I love your taste in

The thing I like to do most with you is

My favorite place to go with you is

You are so smart! You know how to

I love you more than

If you were a type of animal you would be a

If I could buy anything in the world, I would buy you a

You always smell like

I love how you always say

You are as pretty as a

The one thing you are best at is

My favorite outfit that you wear is

You make me happy when you

You win the award for being the best

Made in the USA
Monee, IL
02 May 2022

95784296R00036